Lyric
Words on a Page

TC PELLEGATTA JR.

Cover art: Cy Rae

For all who touched me to all I touched

Dedicated to us

Date, time, temperature and weather conditions listed correspond to the day poems were written

CONTENTS

SOMEDAY YOU'LL MEET A STRANGER WHO IS NOT

22 January 2016
Friday 1410 hrs
Snow 20º

Places to go
People to meet
You never know
Where when
Somehow
Someway
Someday you'll meet a stranger who is not

Walking upper east side 82nd and 3rd
Turned the corner up to Lex Lexington Ave Diner
Place was packed
Not a seat to be had
Turned around to leave
Saw your face
Had that feeling
Don't stand a chance
You never know
Where when
Somehow
Someway
Someday you'll meet a stranger who is not

Help
Please help
Was struck by your beauty
Your name
Could hardly stand
No place to sit
Couldn't be sure
You had to know
Had no way to defend myself
I met the stranger who is not

How lucky can one guy be
One face your face
One in 12 million
Struck me hard
Odds are better winning the lottery
I fell in love with the stranger who is not

THE SIXTIES

21 February 2016
Sunday 0625 hrs
Full moon clear 40º

Alone
A loner
Not lonesome
Drink it snort it
Smoke it
Shoot it
With these four friends
Never alone

Worked uptown
Gordie's Apple Pie 82nd and 3rd
The sixties sexual revolution
The pill was in
Bras came off
Free-wheeling society
No doubt
Through the haze ask myself
Was this real or a dream
4 a.m. time to close
End of the bar a woman sits
Please
I need to go home with you
Thought it was love
Morning she left
Not a word said

Another one-night stand
The sixties sexual revolution

Was young
Handsome
Some said
Hair black
Abs hard
Pocket full of money
Made that night
4 a.m. too early to call it quits
Jump in a limo
Go for ride
Downtown after-hours bar
Drank smoked some more
Tomorrow wake up broke
Another night
Different woman
So many lost count
It wasn't love
Just another day
The 60's sexual revolution

Sex
Drugs
Rock and roll
How it was phrased
Drugs are gone
One night stands
Times have changed
60's gone
Many friends also
I'm alive to spin this yarn
You ask
How could it be
If you remember

The 60's
You weren't there

COUNTRY WOMEN

30 January 2016
Saturday
Cold, Clear 19º

Country women sure are pretty
Two stepping
Sliding around the dance floor
Roadhouse band playing
Lone star beer Jim Beam and coke
How beautiful
Wearing calf-high boots
Short skirt
Lot of leg showing

Job six days a week
Oil field
Working hard
Busting ass
Got a pickup truck
Place to sleep
Beer to drink
Food to eat
Stop at WaWa's on the way home
Buy six-pack
Burrito
Some Skoal
Three major food groups all I need

Boss man
Says

That's it for the day
Jump in my pickup
Can't wait to get home
Smells of corn bread and chicken
Two beautiful children
One on the floor
One on your hip
Long time dreamed of this day
No need to go out
Have it all here
Two-stepping
Sliding around our kitchen floor

RICH MAN LIVING IN POVERTY

03 March 2016
Thursday 1430 hrs
43º

Nothing less
Don't need more
Rich man
Living in poverty
Fast food
Egg sausage cheese
Cup of coffee
One sugar please
First Wednesday third of the month
Automatic deposit
Social security eight hundred sixty four

Homeless young man
Cotton in ears
Eyes intense
Many worse off
Came and went
Finished eating
Ready to leave
Cross street
Buy some grocery
First Wednesday third of the month
Automatic deposit

Social security eight hundred sixty four
Nothing less don't need more
Rich man living in poverty

Lingered a while
Not good
Started to weep
Many people worse off
Hard to watch
Tear filled eyes
Cannot see
Voice says
You alright
Homeless young man
Checking on me
You hungry
Yes
His reply
French fries please
Not enough
To get by
I'm thinking
Third of March automatic deposit
Social security eight hundred sixty four
Nothing but 20s in my pocket
Give one to a man
Worse off

Cross street buy grocery
Four dollars shy
Lady behind
Next in line
I'll pay the difference
Rich man living in poverty

NEVER IS

10 February 1980
Sunday 1101 hrs
Sunny 37º

Sunday it's snowing
Wind blowing
Snow's piled up outside my door
I'm sitting here thinking
Just sitting here thinking
Never is a good time for a broken heart

A snow covered shroud is what I see
I reflect to days
When it was warm
You were lying here
Loving me
With breakfast dishes pushed aside
Paper in total disarray
We looked at each other knowingly
Sunday morning would last all day

Sunday morning lasted all day
You said life together was beautiful
Hoped it would go on and on

The snow is here
You're gone
But the memories linger
And Sunday mornings go on and on

Sunday it's snowing

Wind is blowing
Snow's piled up outside my door
I'm sitting here thinking
Just sitting here thinking
Never is a good time for a broken heart

LYRIC

07 March 2016
Monday 1545 hrs
Clear 40º

What does it mean
Be creative
Write lyric
Words on a page
Can't put it in a book
Shelve it away
Music gives it life
For all to hear

Love me tender
Rock around the clock
Bye bye love
Don't step on my blue suede shoes
Elvis Presley
Bill Haley
Carl Perkins
Chuck Berry
Fats Domino Blueberry Hill
Joni James
Johnny Cash
Buck Owens
Patsy Cline
Ernest Tubb
Willie Nelson
Country music

Rock and roll
Don't need Scotty
From Starship Enterprise
Music will transport you there
Another time
Another day

Take lyric
Add music
Another dimension
Music on the airways
Not in a book shelved away
Childhood
Grade school
Junior high
Time to graduate
Now your wedding day
Music can take you back to another time
Another day

The fifties
Came a new sound
Rock and roll
Parents weren't happy
We went nuts
Pegged pants
Duck's ass hair cut
The sound of the fifties
A generation defined
Sixty years later
It's still here
All started with lyric
Words on a page

NORTH OF NOWHERE

23 April 2017
Sunday 1030 hrs
Clear 52º

Just a little north of nowhere
Missed your call
Miss you
In my thoughts
Often
All these years
No matter how hard I try
Can't get where it used to be
How many times will I hear
Train already left the station
Just found out
No train to Nashville
Might have some coke

Self-inflicted pain
Self-medication sitting at bar
Getting drunk
Need to forget
Juke box playing country music
Pedal steel
Singer singing
"Never is a good time for a broken heart"
Can't recall a conversation with Dr. Leary
Went around the bend
Just a little north of nowhere

Life
On it goes
Many faces
Many places
Few good choices
Many not
Smoking cigarettes
Snorting coke
Drinking champagne
Smoking dope
Got me where I wanted to be
Just a little north of nowhere

More people on this planet every day
Quite okay
Live alone
Just a little north of nowhere

LUDDITE

28 March 2018
Wednesday 1450 hrs
Rain 42º

A luddite
Lost in the past
Don't need broadband
Social media
Smart phone
Android
Tablet
Seventy inch T.V.

A lemming not
Running down the highway
High speed internet
Following all who are lost
Google it
Use G.P.S.
Perhaps you'll find your self

VINCENT & CALI

27 February 2016
Saturday 1139 hrs
42º

Stetson hat
Turned up brim
Brown suede coat
Cool boots
Clear brown eyes
Rimless glasses
I'm Thinking
South Philly
Music dude
Tall
Lean
Good lookin
Hair piled high
Woman at his side
Pen Druid
Sit down
Order beer

Hey man
Where you from
Close by
Warrenton
Cops to it
Yeah I'm a music man
By bus

Travel here, travel there
Sometime
Stay home studio musician
TV show

Middle February
Warm sun
Move outside
Picnic table
Come here Rappahannock County
Meet like minded people
Shahin "Smiggy" Marquisse
Play music
Hit a lick
Eat food
Stay a while

Talked of this
And that
Three days music
Kennedy Center
Louie Bellson
Jerry Mulligan
Duke Ellington
Got on the "A Train" went up town
Quickest way
To get to Harlem
Autographed a book
To Vincent & Cali
Said good bye
We'll meet again
Have beer
On the deck
Pen Druid

CARNEY BROTHERS THREE

25 May 2017
Thursday 1430 hrs
Rain 60º

Once upon a time
Not long ago
Not far away
Small village
Blue Ridge Mountains
Shenandoah Valley
Carney Brothers Three
Open brewery
Pen Druid
The name
People came from far and wide
Drank the brew
Made 'em smile

Children in strollers
Dogs on leashes
Slice RPK pizza
Sign reads
No beer past here
Pot luck
Thursday night
Come have fun
Toss frisbee

Eat food
Stay awhile
Taste life
Rappahannock style

POVERTY

17 October 2017
Tuesday 0900 hrs
Clear 42º

Went to DMV
Get vanity plate
You know the kind
Says something about you
What could that be
For me
I wondered

Long the journey
White hair
Journey brought me here
Place called poverty
Live here
Don't know where

Asked the lady behind the counter could I have
Plate stamped poverty no
She replied
Live in poverty you can't afford this plate

Alas
Didn't get to tell story
With vanity plate
Poverty state of being
Live here
Don't know where

No street address
No telephone
Somewhere called poverty
"Almost"
Reads vanity plate
Where's that
Twelve miles north
Two paychecks from the street
No fixed address
No telephone

BACK ROADS

21 February 2019
Thursday 0500 hrs
Cloudy 38º

Back roads
Forty years
Driven
You laid it open
Revealed your secrets
First flower
Last leaf to fall
Winter snow
Smell spring honeysuckle
Mimosa
Raspberry
Wild roses
Strawberry
Each turn gave more
Grass cut
Smell scallions green grass
Rolling hills
Old Rag on horizon
Horses grazing
Blacksmith shoeing

"INDUSTRIAL GIANT" NO MORE

13 February, 2016
Saturday 0915 hrs
Clear 12º

Once upon a time
Since I can remember
It's the way all stories started
You would have to live it to see how it ended

Born to parents lived in a steel town
Owned a restaurant were independent
Plant operated 24-7
At the top of their game
People got paid a livable wage
Buy a house a car
Send children to college

We went to Japan and Europe
Fight the enemy
Win the war
If you went or stayed home
A price was paid to manufacture machines of war
Years the conflict went on in the end we prevailed

Post war production
Skyscrapers
Bridges railroads built
The nation was hungry for more
Bethlehem didn't think it could roll or make that much steel

Prosperity everywhere
Middle class blue-collar workers were here to stay

Many years the nation rebuilt
Nobody noticed Japan rise from the ashes
They bought our scrap iron ore
Made steel returned to our shores
Tinsel steel we could not weld
Japanese were at the top of their game
Basic oxygen furnace
Continuous cast replaced the open-hearth system
Bethlehem
Giant of production
Shut down
Scrapped out
Shipped to Japan returned as a Toyota van
Makes me sad ashamed of what we've become
You would have to live it to see how it ended once upon a time

WHITE SOCKS LUNCH PAIL

22 October 2018
Monday 1330 hrs
Windy clear 60º

Pennsylvania Lehigh Valley
South Mountain
Nanny Goat Hill
First generation Eastern Block countries
Work Bethlehem Steel
12 years old
Water boy
Working
Open hearth system

Fifty years later
More needed
To retire
Mockeye Kastelnick
Eastern Block country
Joe Sarko
Barney Tuckaush
Pucky Oraveck
White socks
Lunch pail
Color TV

Horn

Siren
Blast
Molten steel feel heat
Four thousand degrees
Twenty thousand ton
Ladle catches all
Many languages spoken
Common thread Eastern Block
Hard working
Nothing free
More hours spent working
Than with family
Maybe die on the job
Work long enough gold watch

Age 25
Many not younger
Many 50 plus 15 more
Work together
Six months plus
Before a return hello
Men Eastern Block country
White socks
Lunch pail
Color TV

Left the steel
White socks
Lunch pail
Color TV
Not for me

JOHNNY

05 February 2016
Monday 0900 hrs
Snowing 12º

Grant Napoleon Eagle
Given name
Call me Johnny he'de say
Worked in shipyard
15 years never missed a shift Friday pay day
He'd go to the Hogg Brothers Honky Tonk
Across from the main gate
Cash his check
Get drunk
Play sad songs on the juke box
Merle Haggard Johnny Cash
Ernest Tubb
Buck Owens Patsy Cline
Sound of pedal steel made him cry
So drunk he couldn't walk
A cab would take him home
Saturday morning woke up broke

Johnny had a wife
Soft spoken
Sweet
Each time he came home drunk
She'd say can no longer live this way
Divorced him once
Hoping it would work

Shortly after married him again
Johnny had three friends
The Hogg Brothers Honky Tonk
Cigarettes and bottle of gin
His sweet wife couldn't take it no more
Divorced him again

Again Johnny was alone
No one to love
Kiss good night
Not all was lost
He had three friends
The Hogg Brothers Honky Tonk
Cigarettes and bottle of gin
No call for a cab that night
Johnny Johnny it's closing time
It's time for you to go

Three a.m. ambulance came
Across from the shipyard's main gate
Where Johnny worked fifteen years never missed a shift
Paper read
He died surrounded by friends
The Hogg Brothers Honky Tonk
Empty table
Half pack of cigarettes and a bottle of gin

SOMETIME

03 May 2018
Wednesday 1300 hrs
Sunny 90º

Sometime
When I treat you
Like you treat me
You don't like the way I treat you

Sometimes
Thinking of sometime
Sometime
It's you
Days gone
Days to come
Life be short
Have fun
Day at a time
More than most can handle
Sun
Always warm

Sometime
Anytime
Been a while
Saw you yesterday

Wanted it

Already had it
Not what I wanted
Greener grass thing

OUT FOXED

02 July 2018
Monday 0800 hrs
Clear 85º

Fall season
Fall color
Slight chill mist hanging
Smell of earth
Hounds baying
Tailgate dropped
Hounds out
Huntsman blowing horn
Ready
Chase
Soon on

Pack of hounds
Riders up dressed to the nines
Excitement running high
Smell
Saddle soap
Braided manes
Tails
Horse coats shine checkerboard pattern on rump
Stirrup cup
Greetings exchanged
Flasks passed around

Gone away
Hounds
Smell fox
Chase on
Ground wet
Scent stays

Sight chase
Hounds noses to ground
Fox clears stone walls
Three strides out
See it unfold
Hilltop hundred yards out

Four hours
Saddle time
Riders dressed to the nines
Pack of hounds
To kennel
Fox in den

SINGER SONG WRITER

20 March 2016
First day of spring
Clear 30º

It's not easy being me
Paper says I'm a singer
Song writer
How can that be
Can't play guitar, sing or carry a tune
One hit wonder
A fluke
Don't know a chord from a key

Like everybody else
I got stories to tell
Just can't get to an instrument
Write a novel
That's out of reach

I'll write lyric
For singer and a band
Inside my mind
It's me live singing on stage
A fantasy land
Singer song writer
So the story goes

Broken heart
Love of my life
Happy once

Now despair
How much better this all sounds
Guitar
Mandolin
Pedal steel
Just ask singer song writer
Willie Nelson
For years lyric sung by others
Patsy Cline falling to pieces
Live inside my mind a fantasy land sit and wonder
What it's like to be a
Singer
Song writer
Live on stage
Singing my lyric
With a band

FORTUNATE MAN

22 March 2016
Tuesday
Spring time 47º

Another sunrise
Another day
I wake up smiling
You're lying next to me
With sandman eyes and pillow wrinkles
You'll look a long time
Find a man more fortunate than me

Won't be long
A limo will come pick me up
To the airport
Another trip
Away from home
Hotels
Motels
Miss my wife miss my kids
Houston
Dallas
Austin
Memphis
Ten more cities
Can't remember
Their names
How many shows
How long will we stay

Writing lyric came easy
Didn't know
How much more it took
Notes chords
Personalities
Studio time when you could get it
How naïve
Really didn't know the difference
Poetry
Prose
Or a song

Days nights are long
The years short
It's hard
When we're apart
On the road
It's all the same
Got home
Kids are grown
In their teens
Thought it was cool come along
See dad rocking and rolling
Performing on stage

Another sunrise
Another day
Wake up smiling
You're lying next to me
With sandman eyes and pillow wrinkles
You'll look a long time
Find a man more fortunate than me

MY DADDY WAS THE SHERIFF

01 May 2016
Sunday
Cold rain 50º

I was born in Southern Virginia
Culpeper that is
Bordered by the counties of Madison and Rappahannock
My daddy was the sheriff
Strict but fair
Small town America
Posted speed limit 25

Grew up
Small town America
Not much to do
Was restless
Had wanderlust
Need to travel
Worked any job
Saved money
Bought an eighteen-wheeler

For years
Need to travel
Couldn't get enough
Hauled steel out of the Northeast
Electric Motors to Syracuse

Drove night and day
Stopped to eat
Small diner
Couple miles north of Tallahassee
Saw your face
It was over
Road never more

Just drive local
Parked my eighteen-wheeler
Seven hundred and fifty thousand miles
Spend every night home
With my wife in our own bed
She writes a column for local newspaper
Small town America my daddy was the Sheriff strict but fair
Posted speed limit 25

SAD COUNTRY SONG

03 January 2016
Sunday 0600
Cold Clear

How many years
How many miles
How many cared

Got home late last night
Million stars in the southern sky
Looked around your car was gone
Not a light on
House was dark
Opened the door
Turned on a light
Empty house
No one home
Faint sound Vince Gill singing on the radio
Kitchen table a note it reads
Could take no more if I don't leave i'll be sorry
When you get home I'll be gone
Not a dream I tell myself
Woke up this morning and you were gone
Like words from a sad country song
Sad country song

Not long ago we were laughing singing not caring
Happy with what life was bringing how long ago
Matters not
Woke up this morning and you were gone

Like words from a sad country song
Sad country song

Doesn't matter where
When I hear our favorite song on the radio
Think of you think of me
How it used to be
Years went by my future spent
Another morning alone
Taste of tears in my throat
How long can I go on
Hard to say
Woke up this morning and you were gone
Like words from a sad country song
Sad country song

GRATITUDE

08 January 2018
Monday 0924 hrs
Cloudy 17º

Coldest winter
In awhile
Temperature and money
At zero
Or below
No water
Pipes frozen
Wood pile almost gone

Two sides of zero
Again
On the wrong side
Social security check twenty six days out
Seventy eight years to get here
Once again
Asking the question
What's gonna happen

Living here
In a place
Like America used to be
Makes one think
I'm richer than you
All you have is money
Wonderful people
Beautiful landscape

Need help
Need not ask
Food Pantry
Benevolent Fund
Here for all who do

Joined the US Marine Corps
05 December 56
Honorable discharge
06 April 64 did what was asked of me
For God and country
"Thank you for your service"
People say
Sixty years hence
Time to say
Thank you
People of Rappahannock for your service
And all that you do

OF ANOTHER TIME

11 January 2018
Thursday 0700 hrs
Cloudy 40º

Small town America
Small town paper
Rappahannock News
Hundred forty years
"All the news that's fit to print"
Written by people you don't know
Here
Not the case
Read the paper
Agree
Disagree
Brack
Clatterbuck
McCaslin
Hardee
See 'em on the street
Discuss it
No fake news

RED RIDER

20 February 2018
Tuesday 1750 hrs
Clear 50º

Blue
Blue eyes
Red hair
Just as red
Paint pony to ride
Come from up Cumberland way
Heather Marsh Turkey Hill Stable
Place to ride

Went out dancing
Dubious Brothers
Road house band playing
Spinning round and round
Got hung up
Chains on her boots
Knocked me to the floor
Bruised her chin
Busted my head

When you coming back
Next week
In a couple weeks
What the hell does that mean
Thanked me for my music
Jumped in rig
West Virginia plates

Gone

VOICE OF AN ANGEL

02 January, 2016
Saturday 1030 hrs
Sunny 42º

Voice of an angel
Some people say when they talk about you
Standing next to you
Asking please sing me a song

Cloudy days
Plenty of snow
Sunshine got its turn
Some rain
Autumn came
Winter too
Thoughts of you keep me warm
Loved you from a distance
You never knew

Thousands came to the show
You sang
You entertained them
Song after song show went on
Applause and tears filled the room
Hard to tell which was greater
Voice of an angel
Audience knew why they came
Center stage you took your bows
Encore
Encore people shouted
With no gas in tank
You sang two more

Heard about your show on radio

Announcer said
Buy your tickets before it's too late
Nashville
Your next gig
Big venue
Could not
Would not miss it
Just had to go
Voice of an angel would be here one time
Man on the radio
Another sold out show
People in the audience
Didn't have a clue
Songs you sang were for me
People holding each other crying
Saying I love you
Encores over
My eyes dry
Could see
On your left finger a wedding ring
Woke up in a sweat
It was all a dream

ENDLESS SUMMER

19 January 2016
Tuesday 1110 hrs
Cold 9º

Summer's day not a cloud in the sky
Sitting here staring at the ocean thinking of you

Spent years together
Endless summer living that dream bonfires on the beach
Sound of surf lapping the shore
You're wonderful
Deeply in love with you

Summer's day not a cloud in the sky
Sitting here staring at the ocean thinking of you

Tan bodies multi-colored beach chairs
Clam bakes
Rock and roll on radio
Drinking beer
Bring back memories all good for sure
Day in day out love was strong

Summer's day not a cloud in the sky
Sitting here staring at the ocean thinking of you

Storm clouds approach
Sky grew dark
Blowing wind
Stinging sand
Umbrellas flew we all ran

Can't remember what happened walked down the beach
Found you in the arms of another man
Endless summer no more

Summer's day not a cloud in the sky
Sitting here staring at the ocean thinking of you

BROKEN HEARTS AND DREAMS

15 January 2016
Friday
Cold 22º

Broken hearts and dreams where do they go
Hopes and dreams had my share look in my mind
Many there

People ask
How you doing
Just a blue-eyed man walking through this world collecting memories
Living a dream
Deep in love walking the beach
High mountain passes
Holding hands
Taste warm kisses
Beautiful face looking back at me

Broken hearts and dreams where do they go
Hopes and dreams had my share look in my mind
Many there

Talk of life together house filled with love and laughter
Children's first step to graduation day collecting memories living a dream

Walking the beach alone

No hand to hold
No warm kisses
Sun goes down
I'm alone
Talk of life together
Was never to be
Broken hearts and dreams
Where do they go
Here
Walking the beach with me

HURTIN’

26 January 2017
Thursday 1315 hrs
Sunny 60º

Get out of my life
Before you hurt yourself again
Your broke your own heart
Can’t blame that hurtin’ on me
We had it all
For you
Not enough

Can’t remember
What year
What chapter
It all came together
Words you said
Many years ago
You broke your own heart
Can’t blame that hurtin’ on me

That sound
That feeling
A song
Remembering
Where
When
With whom
Photographs
Who’s that

Years go by
Hurtin' stays

Cold
Quiet
Dark
Night waits
For morning light
Sound of train whistle
Takes me back
You'd be laying here
Next to me
I'm alone
Still hurtin'

Fool in love
Fool's fool
Fool I am
For you
I'd do it again

PLACE TO BE RAPPAHANNOCK

31 January 2016
Sunday 0520 hrs
Clear 22º

Drive these roads
Walk these streets
Little Washington
Sperryville
Small town America
Rappahannock Co. place to be

People in cars
Pickup trucks
Wave when they go by
Honk the horn
Give a smile
Come to the house
Eat food
Stay a while
Digital age is here
Yet
You can find a woman sitting next to a wood stove
Only source of heat
Sewing
Knitting
Making a quilt
Like America use to be

New year's day

Black eyed peas
Good luck
On the porch Laurel Mills Store
Talking to notables
Stanfield Turner
Tom Brocaw
Lonesome Dove Robert Duvall
If you get here once a year
A warm welcome
From hosts Bill and Mary Francis Fannon

Eating dinner
Thornton River Grille
Cell service
WIFI
Ain't much
Digital age
Not here
No traffic light
Laughter
Talking
People interacting
Imagine a night together without a gadget that has a screen

Cut yesterday
Windrows of hay
Lay
In field
Round bales
Soon will dot landscape
Lucky are we
Cattle
Horses
Sheep
Apples harvested
Cider in the fall
Apple butter
Lions Club
Smell Central Roasters
Roasting the bean

Beautiful

Landscape
People too get hurt
Get sick
You'll see
They'll come help
Wash clothes
Cook food
Clean house
Rides where
When you need to go
Be still
Take time
Heal
Rappahannock
The way America used to be

Old Rag Mountain
Here a billion years
Hike to the top
Look around
See what's here
Before it's gone

LUKE AND MOTORHEAD JOHNNY

14 July 2018
Saturday 1500 hrs
Clear 85º

Luke and Motorhead Johnny
Coast to coast
Twelve speed Volvo
The ride
Amarillo
Place to buy cowboy hat
Luke missing Kathy
Jamie missing Motorhead Johnny

East bound load
Salinas
Nine hundred cases lettuce
Loaded
Driving tandem
Save two days
Non stop
Night and day
Always rolling
Add to bottom line

Luke and Motorhead Johnny
Get along just fine
Truck stop

Not often
Last trip for the month
Watsonville to Jessup
Load of Driscoll strawberries

Luke and Motorhead Johnny
Nine days off
Hanging in Rappahannock County

OLD MAN

25 February 2016
Thursday 0930 hrs
Clear 40º

I'm an old man
Plain to see
Hair is white
Teeth are gone
Dark blue eyes
Now light blue
No money except monthly social security check
Eight hundred sixty four

Want for nothing
Have shelter everything I need
Food pantry provides food
Health is good
UVA doctors and nurses take care of me
Forget not Annie Williams MPT
No money except monthly social security check
Eight hundred sixty four

Living in the country
Rappahannock style twenty miles nearest grocery store
At the end of the month
Will I have money to buy gas for my 1988 For F150 pickup truck
Front Royal is out of reach
Just buy food at Ken Thompson's Corner Store

It's all good
Living in the country
Rappahannock style

Rejoice
Plate is never empty
Take pictures of beautiful landscape
Put in a book for all to share
Singer, song writer
New career what's next
Stay tuned
Old white-haired man
Living in the country
Rappahannock style

You never know who's in the audience
Rappahannock News
Feature story about me
Didn't have a dollar to buy a newspaper

JUST CAN'T TAKE ANOTHER YESTERDAY

01 March 2016
Tuesday
Clear 40º

Today is today
Tomorrow today
Will be yesterday
Early morning
Another day
Without a word you walked away
Just can't take another yesterday

Yesterday
Talk of tomorrow
Promises made
Trips to romantic places
Palm trees
Rum drinks on the beach
Lying in the sand
Steel band playing
Tradewinds blowing
Sail boats on the ocean
Without a word you walked away
Just can't take another yesterday

Tan body
Sand in your hair

Didn't have a care
Deeper in love
Two people could not be
Six o'clock
Sun's coming up
Not a word spoken
Making love on the balcony
Desire got stronger
Couldn't get enough of each other

Boarding pass
21G window seat
Plane climbed fast and high
Soon our playground was out of sight
Rained for days when we got home
Two weeks on the island too short
Tan faded
Promises too
Deep love
Now shallow
House of cards
Nothing left
It's all gone

THE BOOK

19 June 2018
Tuesday 1005 hrs
Clear 90º

Lost and found
Lost again never found
Another chapter
How many more
Long novel
Hope for the best

Book of life
Written on the fly
No rehearsal
Don't be shy
Can't read the last chapter
Not written
Want to know
Who gets the girl
Close my eyes dreams of you
Don't stop
Can't wait
Next chapter

Sunrise
Sweet smell
Honeysuckle
Intoxicating
Taste in throat
Gentle breeze

Mimosa adrift
Kissed your lips
Fell in love
Lost my way

Many years
Many chapters
Still together
Partners for life
Remembering
Smell of honeysuckle
First kiss

Time to leave
Another chapter to write
And they lived happily ever after

LUCKY MAN

18 November 2018
Sunday1823 hrs
Cloudy 37º

Every day walking
Five years
Same shoes
Pronation
Walking on ankles
Lucky man
Have feet
Have shoes

Sign
High school coach's office
Complained
Had no shoes
Saw a man no feet

Told my story
Every day walking
Five years
Same shoes
Pronation
Walking on ankles
How bad is that
Not
Living
Third world country
No clean water

No food
No shelter
Don't beg for food
Have more
Than the need

Rich man
Hiking boots
Tennis shoes
Two days apart
Phone card bonus
Had dinner with Vets
Battle buddy Will King
Army Combat Vet
Harry
In charge
Lady named Shirley

Every day walking
Five years
Same shoes
Pronation
Walking on ankles
Lucky man
Have feet
Have shoes

HUMBLE

24 November 2016
Thursday 0830 hrs
Clear 31º

From the rolling mills of the Bethlehem Steel to the rolling hills of the Shenandoah Valley
All places in between
New York
London
Paris
Athens
Rome
Los Angeles
St. Croix
Washington, D.C.
Saved the best for last
Rural America
Rappahannock County
Billion-year-old mountain
Old Rag the name
To those who came before
Young mountain 19,200 feet tall
Your spirit touches me
I weep

Human race
Arrogant are we

LAST NIGHT

24 October 2017
Tuesday 1510 hrs
Clear 75º

Last night
Long time ago
Loved you forever
Forever became forever it's that long
Since I've seen you

Last night
Our first
And last
Never got better
Our time together
Forever
A long time to wait

Last night
A long time ago
When first we met
Early morn
First light out back door
No looking back can't help it
Think of you every day
All alone
Once again
Older no wiser
A fool looking back
To what once was

A fool in love
A fool's a fool
Once upon a time

SEASONS

18 December 2018
Monday 1300 hrs
Sunny 58º

Winter
Spring
Summer
Fall
Years
Lucky to have ‘em all

Spring
Laying dormant
In Mother Nature’s womb
Child born
Anytime
Spring of life
New beginning
Three season’s to come

Spring
One of four
We get one
Time of innocence
Time of wonder
Time to dream
Time to grow

Summer
Everywhere running free

On the beach
Summer of life
Summer love
Excitement
The first time

Fall
Marriage
Children
A career
Children moved
No need
The space
Sold the house
Got divorced

Winter
Hair
White as snow
Lived four seasons
Time to return
Mother earth
Winter
Spring
Summer
Fall
Years
We're lucky to have 'em all

SPOKEN WORD

02 March 2018
Friday 0930 hrs
Strong winds 40º

March
It's cold
The hawk is out
Indians say
Horses see wind color red
Trees howling
Rivers running strong
Much snow
Another four-cord winter

Winter
Winter of life
Looking back
As far as I can see
All seasons have been good to me

Smoke coming from chimney
Guess the old man's okay
Neighbors
Drive by
Checking on me
Dry wood stacked on porch
Food in the fridge
Gas in the tank
Got my health
Few good friends

What more do I need

Old man of the village
Song writer yes
Singer not
Can't carry a tune
The spoken word

Made in the USA
Middletown, DE
24 July 2019